THE
GREAT
PHILOSOPHERS

Consulting Editors
Ray Monk and Frederic Raphael

Ronald Hayman

....

NIETZSCHE

Nietzsche's Voices

PHŒNIX

A PHOENIX PAPERBACK

First published in Great Britain in 1997 by
Phoenix, a division of the Orion Publishing Group Ltd
Orion House
5 Upper St Martin's Lane
London, WC2H 9EA

Second impression 1999

A catalogue reference is available
from the British Library

ISBN 0 753 80188 4

Typeset by Deltatype Ltd, Birkenhead, Merseyside

Printed in Great Britain by
Clays Ltd, St Ives plc

All translations from the German are by the author.

NIETZSCHE

Nietzsche's Voices

NIETZSCHE'S VOICES

Unless you believe in God, you cannot believe God is dead: an entity which never existed cannot die. Not that Nietzsche ever affirmed unequivocally that he believed God to be dead: he was speaking through the mouth of a madman in an 1882 book, *The Joyful Wisdom*, written, like most of his work, in discontinuous segments. The delicately ambiguous story he titled 'The Madman' is virtually self-contained.

Have you not heard of the madman who lit a lantern in broad daylight, ran to the marketplace and kept crying out: 'Where's God? Where's God?' Because many of the people standing around did not believe in God, there was a good deal of laughter. Has he got lost? asked one. Has he run away like a child? asked another. Or is he hiding? Is he afraid of us? Has he embarked on a ship? Emigrated? There was a good deal of shouting and laughter. The madman rushed into their midst and stared at them. 'Where has God gone?' he cried. 'I will tell you. *We have killed him* – you and I! We are all his murderers. But how have we done it? How could we swallow the sea? Who gave us the sponge to rub out the entire horizon? What were we doing when we unchained the earth from the sun? Where is it going? Where are we going? Away from all suns? Are we hurtling straight downwards? And

3

backwards, sideways, forwards, in all directions? Is there still an up and a down? Are we not drifting through infinite nothing? Is empty space not breathing on us? Has it not got colder? Is night after night not closing in on us? Do we not need lanterns in the morning? Are we still deaf to the noise of the gravediggers digging God's grave? Has the smell of divine putrefaction not reached our nostrils? Gods putrefy too. God is dead! God is still dead! We killed him! How are we going to cheer ourselves up, the worst of all murderers? The holiest and mightiest being in the world bled to death under our knives – who is going to wash us clean of this blood? What kind of water would cleanse us? What festivals of atonement, what penitential celebration will we have to invent? Is the greatness of this deed not too great for us? Shall we have to become gods ourselves to seem worthy of it? No greater deed has ever been done, and whoever is born after us will, thanks to this deed, live in a loftier history than there has ever been.'

The madman now fell silent and looked again at the spectators. They were silent too and stared at him, bewildered. Finally he threw his lantern on the ground, so that it shattered and went out. 'I have come too soon,' he said. 'It is not yet time. This tremendous experience is still on its roundabout way – it has not yet reached the ears of men. To be seen and heard, thunder and lightning need time, the light from the stars needs time, deeds need time, even after they are done. This deed is still more distant than the remotest stars – *and yet they have done it themselves!*'

The Joyful Wisdom, §125

The notion of God's death may have been borrowed from Heinrich Heine's 1834 collection *On the History of Philosophy and Religion in Germany*: 'Our heart is filled with fearful piety. The old Jehovah is preparing for death ... Do you hear the bell tolling? Down on your knees. They are bringing the sacraments to a dying God.' But Nietzsche produced more than a variation on an unoriginal theme. Before introducing the madman, he declared that the greatest danger confronting humanity was 'an eruption of *madness* – an outbreak of arbitrariness in hearing, feeling and seeing; pleasure in mental indiscipline; joy in human unreason'. Like a sleepwalker liable to fall if he wakes, we must go on dreaming there is a reality behind appearances.

For me appearance is what exists and has its effect and mocks itself to such an extent that I feel there is nothing more than appearance, a will o' the wisp, a dance of the spirits – that among the dreamers, even I, the one who knows, am dancing my dance, and that the one who knows is a means of prolonging the terrestrial dance, and therefore belongs among life's masters of ceremony. Perhaps the supreme interconnectedness and consistency of all knowledge will remain the best means of preserving *the continuation of the dream* and the mutual understanding of all dreamers.

The Joyful Wisdom, §54

We could not have survived without our ingrained habit of preferring commitment to uncertainty, error and fiction to doubt, assent to denial, passing judgement to doing justice. Instead of letting scepticism disorient us, we went on clinging to the faith that stabilized us. This is to suggest that only the madman is awake while the sane majority is still dreaming.

The tension in Nietzsche's prose stops us from dismissing the news about God's death as nonsensical babbling. Once the man has accused the people – and himself – of murdering the missing deity, his questions cease to be absurd, while the pounding rhythm stops us from brushing them aside. He is not presented like a fictional character – we get no idea how old he is or what he looks like – but his manner of speaking is different from Nietzsche's.

The prose style is not biblical, while the story is not a parable, but this announcement about the death of the Father could be read as an audacious sequel to the biblical account of the crucifixion. Nietzsche's story is also an early rehearsal for *Thus Spoke Zarathustra*, where both the narrative and the pronouncements of the prophet-like hero depend on pastiche of the Bible.

After Zarathustra had said these words, he fell silent, like one who has not spoken his last word; for some time he weighed his staff doubtfully in his hand. Finally he spoke, and his voice had changed.

And now, my disciples, I am going alone. You should go now too, and alone. This is my wish.

Truly, I exhort you: go from me, and resist Zarathustra. And better still, be ashamed of him. Perhaps he deceived you.

The champion of knowledge must not only love his enemies, he must also be able to hate his friends.

You are rewarding a teacher poorly if you always remain a pupil.

Zarathustra, Part One, 'On the Virtue of Giving'

We hear two voices here, and only one is Zarathustra's. If both are Nietzsche's, both are disguised.

Like Kierkegaard, who made copious use of pseudonyms and personae, Nietzsche was exploring his ambivalence, and nothing provoked more ambivalence in Nietzsche than the religion of his childhood – Lutheran Protestantism. Giving the Germans their first translation of the Bible in 1534, Martin Luther was effectively giving them a national language, imbued with reverence for authority, divine and human. Nothing encouraged artificiality of diction more than the prayer-like piety preachers affected in their sermons and grown-ups in the homilies they directed at children. Elisabeth Foerster-Nietzsche's biography of her brother exemplifies her failure to recover from the linguistic conditioning they both received.

Their father, Karl Ludwig Nietzsche, a Lutheran pastor, died when Friedrich Wilhelm was not yet five, and Elisabeth was three. Seventeen when she married and eighteen when she gave birth to her son, their mother, Franziska Nietzsche, was the daughter of another Lutheran clergyman, while Karl Ludwig's mother, who lived with them and ran the household, regularly overruling her daughter-in-law, was the daughter of an archdeacon and the widow of a superintendent – the equivalent of a bishop. During early childhood Nietzsche had been surrounded by women who had spent their lives with preachers, cooking and housekeeping for them, carrying on conversations with them (probably listening more than talking), emulating them and trying to please them. The moralizing conversational style of these women was modelled on that of their men, and they enjoyed what they took to be a duty – imposing Christianity on the children. Elisabeth, Nietzsche's only sibling to survive, was more conformist by nature. In March 1883, two months after starting *Zarathustra*, he told a friend: *'I do not like my mother and it is painful for me to hear my sister's voice.* I always became ill when I was with them. We have hardly ever quarrelled ... I know how to get on with them, though it does not suit me.'

Throughout his childhood, he had been encouraged by both precept and example to believe that the main function of words was to express reverence. In writing *Thus Spoke Zarathustra*, he was approximating to the idiom, syntax and cadences of the old reverential style, partly to parody them, and partly to construct an echo chamber that would lend extra resonance to the anti-Christian preaching of his pagan prophet.

'Thou shalt not steal! Thou shalt not kill!' – these words were once held to be holy; in front of them knees were bent, heads bowed, and shoes were removed.

But I ask you: has the world ever seen better thieves and killers than these holy words?

Is life not full of stealing and killing? And that these words were held to be holy – did that not kill truth itself?

Or was it the preaching of death that was called holy, which contradicted and went against the whole of life?

8

> Oh, my brothers, break the old tablets of the law for me, break them!
>
> *Zarathustra*, Part Three, 'On the Old Tablets', §10

Statement in Nietzsche's work can never be separated from style, but though he talks to us in a variety of voices, few commentators have offered useful advice on how we should come to terms with this. (The honourable exceptions include Jacques Derrida and Henry Staten, the American author of the book *Nietzsche's Voice*.) Nietzsche comes closer to identifying with Zarathustra than with the madman, but it is not always easy – either with these two voices or with others – to gauge the balance between identification and alienation. The question Staten asks is 'why it's so hard to say who is speaking when "Nietzsche" speaks, who is "I" or "we" and who are "they" in his text.'

It is not only when he is using a persona that we have to confront the problems of voice and tone. The cultivation of different voices and styles was central to his development as a writer and thinker. Only an intensely style-conscious writer would have said, as he did in *Human, All Too Human*, 'To improve your style means to improve your ideas, and nothing else.' Nietzsche's style, as Thomas Mann pointed out, could sometimes be mistaken for that of Oscar Wilde. Either of them could have written: 'It is only shallow people who do not judge by appearances.' Nietzsche, the author of that sentence, also said: 'It is only as an *aesthetic phenomenon* that existence and the world are permanently *justified*.'

This orientation towards the aesthetic gave him something in common with Wilde, but according to an 1888 note, written just before Nietzsche's breakdown into insanity, 'For a philosopher to say "the good and the beautiful are the same" is infamy; if he then adds "Also the true", he ought to be thrashed. Truth is ugly. We possess *art* lest we *perish of the truth*.'

Here it is only the last two sentences that could be translated into a Wildean idiom. Generally, Nietzsche's aphorisms are less often reminiscent of Wilde's than of Wittgenstein's. As Erich Heller shows in an essay, 'Wittgenstein and Nietzsche', it would be easy to take a pronouncement by one for a pronouncement by the other, though, in the 1920s Wittgenstein had not yet caught up with Nietzsche's 1873 essay 'On Truth and Falsehood in an Extra-Moral Sense', which contends that language cannot convey the objective truth about external reality. Since we cannot help being defrauded, we have evolved linguistic conventions to defraud ourselves reassuringly. Nietzsche compared language to a prison-house and to a net; Wittgenstein spoke of its 'bewitchment of our intelligence' and of 'bruises which the understanding has suffered by bumping its head against the limits of language'.

Sometimes Nietzsche's aphorisms are less reminiscent of Wilde or Wittgenstein than of Kafka, who said we are nihilist thoughts in the mind of God. Nietzsche, who regarded God's death as tantamount to a second Fall of Man, suggested that in our second expulsion we must see the promise of a new paradise, for 'the Devil may start to envy those who suffer too deeply and throw them out – into Heaven'.

Like Kafka, Nietzsche was a deeply religious unbeliever. But, together with many of the other notes collected posthumously in *The Will to Power*, this beautiful paradox suggests that, functioning more like a creative writer than a philosopher, he sometimes jotted down phrases because of their verbal appeal, not asking himself until later what they meant and whether he agreed with them. Writing was often like taking dictation from an internal voice.

To explain why he functioned in the way he did, we could start with his infirmity. Both his habits of thinking and his methods of working were affected by the disease that dogged him. Throughout his twenty-three years of adult sanity – he was forty-four when he went mad – he was fighting against long-lasting headaches, pain in and around the eyes, stomach cramps, dizziness, nausea, insomnia, indigestion, neurasthenia. He never found out what was making him ill. With astonishing patience and dwindling optimism, he wandered from place to place, following suggestions from doctors and friends, searching for a climate that would alleviate the symptoms.

His greatest limitation was that he could not sustain any activity – reading, writing or even thinking – over long periods. His work had to be done in snatches. If he read or wrote for too long at a stretch, his eyes gave him more pain than he could bear. Sometimes they hurt so much that he had to lecture without notes, and to dictate instead of writing. Much of his best thinking was done when he was in the open air. As a philosopher he was less suited to long-distance running than to sprinting.

He often made jottings on scraps of paper, and the style of these jottings often survived in both lectures and essays, but if his books seem more disjointed and impressionistic than

11

those of his contemporaries, they also seem more modern. Most of the great nineteenth-century German philosophers were more systematic in their thinking, more inclined to system-building and abstraction. It may have been lack of stamina that led Nietzsche to organize his books in relatively brief units, or it may have been intuitive insight into the value of discontinuity. In either case the fragmentation worked hand in hand with his assumption that philosophy should concern itself with the minutiae of human behaviour. Writing his impressionistic historical commentaries, he could isolate contradictions and moments of disjunction instead of focusing, as most contemporary historians did, on personalities, trends, and periods circumscribed by dates. As a historian, he was brilliant, if erratic. His poor eyesight stopped him from reading enough to substantiate all the sweeping generalizations he made, while many of his scientific and theological arguments were based more on inspired guesswork and acute self-observation than on reading or research; but in tracing the genealogy of morality and in analysing the psychology of punishment, he substantially anticipates Michel Foucault's 1975 book *Discipline and Punish: The Birth of the Prison*. Nietzsche noticed, for instance, how disciplinary systems function on the assumption that wrongdoers become debtors to the community. The creditor – church or state – must be allowed to demonstrate its power by inflicting pain and humiliation on the culprit. In this way accounts are balanced.

Coleridge praised the 'men in all ages who have been impelled as by an instinct to propose their own nature as a problem, and who devoted their attempts to its solution'.

Malaise can tend to focus consciousness on its own functioning, and, like Dostoevsky and Proust, Nietzsche had a genius
for turning introspection outwards, using his consciousness
as an observation base for venturing into generalization
about the human mind and its workings.

Physical discomfort intensified the feeling of being divided
within himself, but this was in some ways advantageous.
Without self-division, he said, there is no self-analysis, while,
magnifying the self-division, his self-analysis also enlarged it.
Instead of listening to one internal voice, he listened to
several, and disagreements between them were often vehe-
ment. But though there is an element of self-dramatization
in his writing, he did not function like a dramatist. A play by
Nietzsche is as unthinkable as one by Immanuel Kant or
John Bunyan: Nietzsche's relationships with his voices were
not like a playwright's with his characters. When Nietzsche
heard voices in his head, he was less interested in reproduc-
ing the conflict than in dramatizing the process of self-
conquest that seemed to be going on ceaselessly inside him.
The main drive was towards monologue, not dialogue.
Zarathustra has various interlocutors, but there is little
interaction with them. Nietzsche wanted to be a law-breaker,
to dethrone the judge, bury the god, take control of the
didactic voice he could never silence.

Discussing the multiplicity of voices in his prose, Henry
Staten refers to what Derrida called 'the Nietzsches' – the
voices in his text that sometimes contradict each other.
Staten diagnoses a 'nostalgia for a lost unity'. Nietzsche's
writings on rhetoric describe a primal mythological being
with a hundred heads that could talk to each other. Realiz-

ing that this dialogue could continue, the creature let itself disintegrate into individual men, knowing it could not altogether lose its unity. Nietzsche liked this idea that we are all fragments of what was once an enormous creature.

Condemning Wagner as 'the modern artist par excellence', he complained that the problems presented in the operas (or 'music-dramas') were all problems of the hysteric. One of the notes collected in *The Will to Power* defines the hysteric as 'admirable in every art of dissimulation'. Vanity and irritability make him dramatize every trivial incident and minor accident. No longer an individual, he is more like 'a rendezvous of individuals – first one and then another shoots forward with shameless assurance'. Staten notices how close this is to the passage in *Twilight of the Idols* describing the 'Dionysian state', which excites the affective system into 'driving forth simultaneously the power of representation, imitation, transfiguration, transformation, and all kinds of mimicry or acting'. The significant element is 'the inability *not* to react (as in certain hysterics who also, on any prompting, enter into *any* role ... they constantly transform themselves)'. Though Nietzsche would have enjoyed neither being compared with Wagner nor being classed as a hysteric, the affinity between the two passages, does, as Staten argues, throw light on the problem of the multiple voices.

Alternatively, we could look at them in a Jungian perspective. As a nineteen-year-old medical student, Carl Jung attended séances at which a fifteen-year-old cousin, Helene Preiswerk, was the medium. Entering the trance state, she went pale as she sank into a chair or onto the floor, drew several deep breaths and began to talk in the person of dead relatives, speaking in high German instead of her normal Swiss dialect. Sounding older and more experienced than she was, while moving more gracefully than usual, she convinced Jung that the voices of his two grandfathers were speaking through her. Six years later, writing his dissertation, he said the voices represented fragments of her own personality that had been 'split off'.

Assuming that the emotions which came into play had been repressed, he applied Freud's term 'hysterical identification' to the 'hysterical delirium' in which Helene's dream fantasies 'became typical hallucinations'. Pathological liars who get swept away by their fantasies, he says, behave like children who get lost in a game or like actors who surrender to their roles. (Jung, *Collected Works*, Vol. 1, p.67) This is not unlike Nietzsche's account of the hysterical histrionics in Wagner's work, and though Nietzsche was at first in control of his voices, he lost control when he went mad.

The fear of madness was not always entirely separate from anxiety that without God, civilization would disintegrate. Dostoevsky resembled Nietzsche both in being deeply religious by temperament and in being apprehensive about the consequences of nihilism. If God is alive, everything is meaningful; if God is dead, everything is permissible and nothing is comprehensible. 'I made up my mind long ago not to understand,' says Ivan Karamazov. 'If I try to understand anything, I shall be false to the fact, and I am determined to stick to the fact.' So was Nietzsche.

Schiller's 1795–6 essay 'On Naive and Reflective Poetry' praises the Greek poets for being effortlessly at one with nature. Against this Rousseauistic Romanticism, Nietzsche argued that naive art always represents a triumph of Apollonian order over Dionysian turbulence. Dionysian art makes us look confidently into the horrors of existence, empathizing with primordial being in its rage for life and its terror at impending destruction. Nietzsche equated the Dionysian with the superabundance of creative energy that foments 'desire for *destruction*, change and becoming'. Or, as Zarathustra is made to put it, 'Whoever wants to be a creator in good and evil, he must first be an annihilator and destroy values.'

In an 1885 notebook Nietzsche described the Dionysian as 'that acme of joy at which a man can feel apotheosized, can feel that Nature is justifying itself in him'. But the 'slaves of "modern ideas", the children of a fragmented, pluralistic, sick, weird period' had lost the capacity for happiness the Greeks possessed. Without it they could not have participated in Dionysian festivals: the Hellenic soul had flourished without any need for morbid exaltation or madness. And in a notebook he kept from March to June 1888, the last year of his sanity, Nietzsche defines the Dionysian as

> a drive towards unity, reaching beyond personality, the quotidian, society, reality, across the chasm of transitoriness: an impassioned and painful overflowing into darker, fuller, more buoyant states; an ecstatic affirmation of the totality of life as what remains constant – not less potent, not less ecstatic – throughout all fluctuation; the great pantheistic sharing of joy and distress which blesses and endorses even the ghastliest, the most questionable

16

elements in life; the eternal will for regeneration, fruitful-
ness, recurrence; the awareness that creation and destruction are inseparable.

The Will to Power, §1050

To say that Nietzsche cultivated disconnectedness within
the self is to say that he was consciously risking destruction –
disintegration. 'Dionysus cut to pieces is a promise of life; it
will constantly be reborn, constantly return from destruction.' As Plutarch explained in his account of this alternative
creation myth, the god was dismembered, but his parts were
distributed into winds, water, earth, stars, planets, animals.
The story serves as the basis for seasonal allegories in which
wintry destruction and death are followed by regeneration,
but it was dangerous for a man to emulate a god.

Nietzsche passed on his early ideas of self-division and
internal conflict to Zarathustra:

And life itself told me this secret: 'Behold,' it said, 'I am
that which must always conquer itself.'

Indeed you call it the creative drive or the compulsion
to achieve something more exalted, remote or complex,
but all this is the same – and the same secret.

I would rather go under than give up this one precept,
and truly, where there is decay and leaves are falling,
behold, life is sacrificing itself – for power!

That I must be struggle, and becoming, and objective
and resistance to the objective – oh, those who discover
my intention will discover what *crooked* paths they must
tread.

Whatever I create and however much I love it – I must

17

soon go against it and against my love. That is what my willpower wills.

You too, truth-seeker, are only a path and a footprint of my will. Truly, my will to power walks on the heels of your will to truth...

Truly, I tell you good and evil exist only temporarily. They must conquer themselves again and again, drawing on their own resources.

You lovers of words, you are being violent with your values and your sayings about good and evil, and that is your secret love, and the brilliance, trembling and overflowing of your souls.

But a greater force is growing out of your values, and a new conquest in which egg and shell are shattered.

And he who will create in good and evil, truly he must be a destroyer first, and smash values.

So the greatest evil belongs to the greatest goodness, but that is what is creative...

Zarathustra, Part Two, 'On Self-Conquest'

Nietzsche may have been unaware of the extent to which Zarathustra was echoing Wagner's Wotan, who was 'eternally sickened to find nothing but myself in everything I bring about ... Whatever I love I have to abandon, those whom I woo I murder, deceitfully betray whoever trusts me ... destroy what I have built ... My work I abandon. I want only one thing – the end.' (Wagner, *The Valkyries*, Act II, sc. 2)

But Zarathustra is more Dionysian than Wagnerian, and the whole story of Nietzsche's development could be told in terms of his relationship with Dionysus. His first book, *The Birth of Tragedy from the Spirit of Music* (1870–1), insists that between the orderly Apollonian tendency and the disorderly Dionysian tendency, there was no enmity. They 'walk together side by side … inciting each other to increasingly powerful births' that culminate in the birth of Greek tragedy, which is no more Apollonian than Dionysiac. At Pforta, Germany's most illustrious classical school, where the boys spent ten or eleven hours each week on Latin and six on Greek, learning not only to read but also to speak both languages, Nietzsche developed a lifelong passion for classical culture and especially for Greek tragedy. In his early enthusiasm for Wagner, Nietzsche regarded him as a genius who could fuse music and drama together – a prodigious cultural achievement that would have the effect of launching Germany into a new renaissance and reuniting art with philosophy after two thousand years of divorce.

Though he found it hard to wean himself away from Wagner's influence, Nietzsche made the break during his early thirties, and in his 1877 book, *Human, All Too Human*, he tries to steer away from the heroic towards the quotidian. He wanted to observe human behaviour 'scientifically', concentrating on 'the small inconspicuous truths'. He had received no formal training as a philosopher, and it had struck him that in the German tradition the philosophical dogmatists – not only idealists but materialists and realists – had all concerned themselves with problems irrelevant to everyday living.

Academically, he had moved from classics to philology, and he was only twenty-four in 1869 when he took up an appointment as professor at Basel University. But his poor health forced him to stop teaching in 1876. The most analytical of philologists, he became extraordinarily sceptical about language, and if Roland Barthes is right to contend that 'the invention of a paradoxical discourse is more revolutionary than provocation', Nietzsche became a revolutionary in 1873 when, still a professor at the university and still suffering from the eye trouble that had been forcing him to lecture without notes, he dictated an essay on language and objectivity – 'On Truth and Falsehood in an Extra-Moral Sense'.

Language, he argued, was like an umbrella: we hold it up to shield ourselves from awareness that the universe is at best indifferent and at worst hostile. Words can never be transparent

> for between two absolutely disparate spheres such as subject and object there can be no connections which are causal, precise or expressive, but nothing more than an *aesthetic* interaction, I mean the transmission of hints, a stumbling translation into a wholly foreign language, for which we invariably need a freely poeticizing and freely inventive intermediate faculty and intermediate area.

> The insect and the bird perceive a different world from ours, and we should not congratulate ourselves on having better vision, for there is no standard of comparison. A poor man can mislead us by pretending to be rich, but what does *rich* mean? All our words are based on equations between unequal things, and they can never have more than a tenuous relation to what they represent.

Because men want – out of necessity and boredom – to exist socially and as part of the herd, they need an armistice and try to get rid of at least the crudest sort of war in which everyone is against everyone else. This armistice entails something that looks like the first step towards satisfying that enigmatic drive towards truth. Something will now be fixed that should from now on be 'truth': what is invented, in other words, is a standardizing, valid and compulsory designation of things, and this linguistic legislation also lays down the first laws of truth, for what is now coming into existence is a differentiation between truth and falsehood. The liar uses valid descriptions – words – to make the unreal appear real; he says for example 'I am rich' when 'poor' would be the accurate description of his situation. He misuses fixed conventions by convenient alteration or even inversion of the names. If he does this in a way that serves his own interest at the expense of other people's, society will no longer trust him and will want to banish him. Men object not so much to being deceived as to being harmed by deception ... Their desire for truth is similarly limited: their desire is for the pleasant consequences of truth which are conducive to survival, but they are indifferent to the perception of truth for its own sake, and hostile to truths that might be dangerous or damaging...

So what is truth? A mobile army of metaphors, metonyms, anthropomorphisms – in short an aggregate of human relationships which, poetically and rhetorically heightened, become transposed and elaborated, and which, after protracted popular usage, pose as fixed,

canonical, obligatory. Truths are illusions whose illusori-
ness is overlooked.

On Truth and Falsehood in an Extra-Moral Sense, §1

Already, at the beginning of his philosophical work,
Nietzsche had arrived at an impasse. Without words, he had
no way of communicating with his readers, and words were
unreliable. How was he to go on? One advantage of speaking
through a persona was that readers would have to think
twice about whether to believe that he believed what the
persona was saying.

Thus Spoke Zarathustra is the most impressive – and the
longest sustained – of all Nietzsche's experiments in mimick-
ing other voices and writing in styles that did not come
naturally to him. While he used the madman only in the one
sequence, he went on speaking through the mouth of
Zarathustra in four successive books, spread over more than
two years.

Both the narrator's voice and the voice of Zarathustra were
intended to drown out echoes of the moralizing voices that
had dominated Nietzsche's childhood, but his work on the
book was precipitated by the experience of falling in love for
the first time at the age of thirty-seven. Charismatic, good-
looking, strong-willed and highly intelligent, Lou Salomé
was the twenty-one-year-old daughter of a Russian general.
Nietzsche met her on a visit to the Italian lakes, where he was
soon having fantasies about her as his daughter, pupil and
spiritual bride. She thought he might one day reveal himself
as the prophet of a new religion, and it was mainly about

religion that they talked, spending, she said, ten hours a day in conversation.

He fantasized about forming a non-sexual *ménage à trois* with her and the young author of a book called *Psychological Observations*, Paul Rée, who had introduced him to her. But this was not a practicable plan, and frustration took a heavy toll on Nietzsche's ailing constitution. 'Unless I can learn the alchemist's trick of turning this filth into gold,' he wrote, 'I am lost.' His crucible was his mind, and it took only ten frenzied days to distil the first book of *Zarathustra* out of the filth. He slipped easily into both the persona and the style. His urge for vengeance was irrepressible, but the main drive was towards gaiety. 'It is not anger but laughter that is lethal,' says Zarathustra. 'Let us kill this gravity.'

Zoroaster (*Zarathustra* in German) was the founder of a pre-Islamic Persian religion in the sixth century BC. He refined the old Aryan folk religion with his idea of eternal punishment according to the balance between good and evil deeds on earth. For Nietzsche he represented the values of good and evil in humanity's oldest stories, and Nietzsche developed his creative fantasy of the prophet Zarathustra as his son after abandoning his self-indulgent fantasy of Lou as his daughter.

The negative experience had to be transformed into something positive enough to inflame other people. He must look down into the abyss and make it ring with defiant laughter, equating Lou and Rée, who had gone off together, with life in the big city. The image of flies in the market place is used to vilify social life. 'Escape, my friend, into your

23

solitude, where the air is fresh and strong.' High altitude represents the alternative to city life – withdrawal, detachment, meditation, peace, solitude. 'He who climbs the greatest mountains can laugh at all tragedies and all tragic seriousness.'

Listening to the argumentative voices inside his head, Nietzsche brought himself back into a state of equilibrium by what we might call sleight of ear. Arguing with himself about Lou Salomé, Paul Rée, life, love, Jesus, God and humanity, he heard a didactic voice calling him to order, and he could write well enough to translate this voice into that of Zarathustra. Soon he had acquired enough confidence to preach through Zarathustra's mouth.

Of all that has been written I love only what men have written with their blood. Write with blood, and you will find that blood is spirit.

It is not easy to understand the blood of others: I hate lazy readers.

Know your reader, and you will do nothing more for him. Another century of readers, and spirit itself will stink.

If everyone must learn to read, it is not only writing that will be ruined in the long run but also thinking.

Once spirit was God, then it became a man, and eventually a mob.

He who writes in blood and proverbs wants not to be read but learned by heart.

In the mountains, the shortest route is from peak to peak, but you need long legs. Proverbs should be peaks, and the audience should have grown tall.

The air thin and pure, danger near and the spirit full of cheerful malice: these things are in tune.

I want goblins around me, for I am bold. Boldness, which scares spirits away, calls up goblins – boldness wants to laugh.

I no longer share your feelings: these clouds I see under me, black and heavy, they make me laugh but for you they are thunder clouds.

You look upwards when you want to be uplifted. I look downwards because I have been.

Which of you can laugh and be uplifted at the same time?

…Wisdom wants us to be brave, unconcerned, playful, violent. She is a woman and loves only warriors…

I would believe only in a God who could dance.

And as I saw my Devil, he was serious, earnest, profound, solemn; he was the spirit of gravity – everything falls through him…

I have learnt how to walk: now I can run. I have learnt how to fly: now I can move forwards without being pushed.

Now I am light, I am flying, I see myself underneath me, now a God is dancing through me.

Thus spoke Zarathustra.

Zarathustra, Part One, 'On Reading and Writing'

Instead of blessing the meek, the merciful and the peace-lovers, Zarathustra favours the great despisers, those who 'do not want to have too many virtues'. He rejects the Christian ideal of brotherly love. 'Your love for your neighbour is only love for yourself.' More has been accomplished by bravery and warfare than by neighbourly love. 'You say that a good cause justifies even war? ... I say unto you: it is a good war that justifies any cause.' But, seeing that this dictum could be used in militaristic propaganda, Nietzsche attacks nationalism: 'State is the name of the coldest of cold monsters. Coldly it tells lies ... in all the tongues of good and evil ... It bites with stolen teeth, and it bites readily.' Reversing both the Mosaic principle of demanding an eye for an eye, a tooth for a tooth, and the Christian principle of turning the other cheek, Zarathustra advises the adder to take back its poison, since it cannot afford to lose it.

> But if you have an enemy, do not repay evil with good, for that is shaming. Rather show that he did something good to you ... It is nobler to declare oneself wrong than right, especially when one is right, only one must be rich enough for that. I do not like your cold justice. The eye of the judge glints with the cold steel of the executioner.

Nietzsche now resumed the *motif* of God's death.

> It was all over a long time ago for the old gods, and truly it was a fine goodbye.
>
> Their death had nothing to do with twilight – that was a lie. The truth is that they killed themselves with *laughter*!
>
> That happened when the most godless words were uttered by one of the gods – the words: 'There is *one* God. Thou shalt have no other God beside me.' – a grim old greybeard of a god, a jealous god, forgot himself in this way.

> Then all the gods laughed and rocked on their chairs
> and called out: 'Is this not what divinity is – that there are
> gods but no God?'
>
> *Zarathustra*, Part Three, 'On Apostasy'

Though he strongly preferred polytheism to monotheism, Nietzsche felt less hostile to God than to the men who had used him to prop themselves up. Zarathustra is made to encounter the last Pope:

> He saw someone sitting beside the path he was taking – a
> tall, black man with a lean, pale face. Repelled, he said in
> his heart: 'Oh dear, there is calamity in disguise, looking
> like a priest. What does he want in my kingdom?'...
>
> 'Whoever you are, wanderer,' he said, 'help a man who
> has lost his way, a seeker, an old man who could easily
> come to harm here.
>
> To me this world is strange and remote. I heard wild
> animals howling, and the man who might have protected
> me is himself no more.
>
> I was looking for the last pious man, a saint and hermit
> who 'isolated in his forest' had still not heard what the
> whole world now knows.'
>
> '*What* does the whole world now know?' asked Zara-
> thustra. 'You mean that the old god is no longer alive in
> whom the world once believed?'
>
> 'That is so,' said the old man, troubled. 'And I served
> this old god to his last hour.
>
> Now I have no employment, no master, but I am not
> free, and never happy except in my memories.
>
> That is why I climbed these mountains, that at last I

might again have a festival, as befits an old pope and father of the church – you should know that I am the last pope! – a festival of pious memories and divine service.'...

'You served him to the very end?' asked Zarathustra thoughtfully, after a long silence. 'Do you know *how* he died? Is it true, as they say, that he was choked by pity – that he saw how *man* was crucified, and could not bear it, that love of mankind was his hell and finally his death?'

But instead of answering, the old pope looked away with a pained and grim expression.

'Let him go,' said Zarathustra after prolonged reflection, constantly looking straight into the old man's eyes.

'Let him go, he has gone. And although it does you credit that you still say only good things of the one who is dead, you know as well as I *who* he was and how strange his ways were.'

'Only these three eyes must see this,' said the old pope more cheerfully (for he was blind in one eye) 'but I am more informed about God's affairs than Zarathustra himself, and so I should be.

He had my love at his disposal for many long years, my will followed only his. But a good servant knows everything, and many things too that his master conceals from himself.

He was a secretive god, given to stealthiness. Truly, he was deceitful even about having a son. Adultery stands in the doorway of his religion.

Those who glorify him as a god of love set too little value on love itself. Did this god not want to be a judge as well? But to love is to go beyond reward and punishment.

When he was young, this god from the Orient was harsh and vindictive, and he built a hell for the entertainment of his favourites.

But in the end, he was old and soft and mellow and compassionate, more like a grandfather than a father, but most of all like a doddering old grandmother.

So he sat feebly in his inglenook corner, fretting about his weak legs, weary of the world and weary of exerting willpower, and choked one day on his all-too-great compassion.'

Zarathustra, Part Four, 'Without Employment'

Feeling more at home than ever before in a mask or an alien style, Nietzsche could write more autobiographically, indulging the inclination to dramatize his own situation. Having fewer friends and less contact with them as he grew older, he felt this need all the more keenly. Zarathustra inherits both Nietzsche's solitude and his peripatetic restlessness:

I am a wanderer, he said to his heart, and a mountainclimber. I am no lover of the plains, and it seems I cannot sit still for long.

And whatever is still to come by way of fate and experience, it will include wandering and climbing mountains: in the end a man's experience is only himself.

The time has passed when accidents could still befall me, and what *could* happen to me now that is not already mine?

It only returns, finally comes home to me – my own self,

and what was long in faraway places, scattered among things and events.

And I know something else: I am now standing in front of my final peak, the one that has waited for me the longest time. Oh, I must start the hardest of my journeys, begin the loneliest of my wanderings.

But one who is like me cannot escape this moment, the moment that tells him: 'Now at last you are on your way to greatness. Mountain-tops and valleys are joined together.'

Zarathustra, Part Three, 'The Wanderer'

Zarathustra also inherits Nietzsche's defiant masochism. Too impoverished to pay for comfortable accommodation or for enough heating in winter, he tries to take control of his ill-fortune by fighting against himself and with the forces that seem hostile.

I am Zarathustra the godless, I boil every misfortune in my pot, and only when it has been thoroughly cooked do I welcome it as *my* food.

And truly, many events have come to me arrogantly, but my will spoke to them more arrogantly still, until they were on their knees, begging –

Begging for heart and hearth, and flattering me: 'Look, Zarathustra, how only a friend comes to a friend!'

But what am I saying when no-one has ears like *mine*. And this is what I will shout to the winds:

You become smaller and smaller, you small people! You are fading away, you lovers of the easy life! You are being destroyed.

> By your many little virtues, by your many little sins of omission, by your resignation.
>
> Your soil is too protective, too yielding. For a tree to become tall, it must grow tough roots among hard rocks.
>
> Zarathustra, Part Three, 'Before Sunrise'

Zarathustra feels disgusted by what normally arouses happiness.

> What is the greatest experience? It is the hour of great contempt ... when you say 'What does my happiness matter? It is poverty and filth and pitiful contentment ... I love all those who do not know how to live except by going under, for they are the ones who go over.'

This apparent indifference to happiness did not make Nietzsche anti-physical.

> The mature and enlightened say 'I am wholly body and nothing else; soul is only a word for something about the body.' ... Behind your thoughts and feelings, my brother, stands a mighty ruler, an unknown sage called Self. He inhabits your body, he is your body.

There is no direct dramatization of the frustrating experience with Lou Salomé and Paul Rée, but Zarathustra warns his disciples against women.

> Is it not better to fall into the hands of a murderer than into the fantasies of a lecherous woman?
>
> But look at those men – their eyes tell you that they know of no greater pleasure than to lie by a woman's side...

Do I recommend chastity? With some, chastity is a virtue, but with most, nearly a vice.

Is it true that they abstain, but the bitch sensuality looks enviously out of everything they do...

And how gracefully the bitch sensuality knows how to beg for piece of spirit when denied a piece of flesh!

Zarathustra, Part One, 'On Chastity'

Of course, there is no explicit discussion in *Zarathustra* of the autobiographical element in philosophy, but in *Beyond Good and Evil* Nietzsche writes:

I have gradually come to understand what every great philosophy until now has been: the confession of its author and a kind of involuntary unconscious memoir. At the same time the moral (or immoral) intentions in each philosophy have constituted the real seed from which the entire plant has grown. Indeed, the best (and cleverest) way to explain how a philosopher arrived at his most obscure metaphysical assertions is to ask: what morality is he aiming at? This is why I do not believe that philosophy originated out of a 'drive to knowledge', but that here, as elsewhere, another drive has exploited knowledge (and misinformation) as mere tools. But anyone who studies man's fundamental drives to see how far they have been at work here as *inspiring* spirits (or demons or goblins) will find that they have all been philosophical at some stage, and that each one of them would be only too glad to present *itself* as the ultimate purpose of existence and as the *master* of all the other drives. For each drive wants to be dominant, and philosophizes as if it were ... Nothing at all about the philosopher is impersonal; above all his morality provides decided and decisive evidence about *who he is* – i.e. the relative positioning of the innermost drives in his nature.

Beyond Good and Evil, §6

He also says in *Beyond Good and Evil* that 'the degree and kind of a man's sexuality reach up into the ultimate pinnacle of his spirit.' (§75) But in *Zarathustra* the generalizations about women and sexuality often seem out of character – acidified by the wound Lou had inflicted on Nietzsche. 'A real man wants danger and sport, so he wants the most dangerous plaything there is – woman.' 'You are going to see women? Do not forget your whip.'

Venturing so far away from all the old norms, Nietzsche was driving his powers of reasoning into the danger zone where madness could overtake him. Scared of it, he tries to accommodate his anxiety in the narrative. 'Write with blood, and you will find that blood is spirit … I have learned to walk, so I let myself run. I have learned to fly, so I do not let myself be pushed.' 'I say unto you: to give birth to a dancing star, one must have chaos within oneself.'

In one sequence a jester follows a trapeze artist onto a rope and jumps over him, making him lose his balance and fall. The incident is puzzling, but one interpretation is suggested when Zarathustra says that while there are many ways of conquering oneself, only a jester would try to skip over Man. Another is that Nietzsche is counting on the character he had created, Zarathustra, to save him from losing his balance.

33

In a letter about the poems or 'Dionysus songs' he was writing, he called them 'the latest form of my madness'.

But he no longer wanted his feet to stay prosaically on the ground: 'I want to make things *as hard* for myself as they have ever been for anybody: only under this pressure do I have a *clear* enough conscience to possess something few men have or have ever had – *wings*, so to speak.'

His appetite for self-conquest was insatiable. 'And life itself did tell me this secret: "Behold," it said, "I am that *which must always conquer itself* ... and truly, where there is decline and the falling of leaves, behold, life is sacrificing itself – for power."' Caught in the cross-fire of Nietzsche's battle against himself, the reader cannot afford to ignore the warning: 'And you too, truth-seeker, are only a path and a footprint of my will. Truly, my will to power walks on the heels of your will to truth.'

Having lent his voice to a madman when he announced the death of God, Nietzsche now uses Zarathustra to introduce the concept of the *superior man* (*Übermensch*). The point is to suggest that human potential can be realized more fully. Mistranslated as 'Superman', the word *Übermensch* has confused modern readers, who have lost sight of the Darwinian perspective in which Nietzsche was writing. Schopenhauer had suggested that the greatest men formed 'a kind of bridge across the turbulent stream of becoming', and in 1873, nearly ten years before he started *Zarathustra*, Nietzsche had written: '*The goal of humanity* cannot be located in its end but *in its finest specimens*.' (*The Uses and Disadvantages of History*)

Believing that the quality of life was steadily improving, he credited this to the outstanding men of each generation. By

1883 he had become less optimistic, but to him, the idea of the superior man was already so clear that the only definition he provides is negative and indirect – based on the vague phrase *all-too-human*: 'Truly, even the greatest men I found all-too-human.' What humanity needs is men who will do better by using the dialectic of conflict and self-conquest that culminates in self-transcendence. Those with enough strength, says Zarathustra, should imitate the virtues of a marble column, which becomes finer, gentler and internally harder as it ascends. Those who are elevated will become beautiful and shudder with godlike desires, their vanity imbued with adoration.

After completing *Zarathustra* in 1885, when he was forty, Nietzsche never again sustained an impersonation for so long. It could be said that in adopting so many voices and styles he was flirting with madness, but it could equally well be argued that without the voices he could not have held madness at bay so long. Most writers think they know what they mean when they say 'I'; more sophisticated and less superficial, Nietzsche was more vulnerable, though he did not explore the dangers until he wrote *Beyond Good and Evil*: *Prelude to a Philosophy of the Future*, which he started in the summer of 1885 and completed early in 1886.

Aware that he would no longer be protected by a mask, he had decided to confront all the implications of what he had written in 1873 about the impossibility of using words to tell the truth. For thirteen years, sidestepping many of the issues, he had never abandoned the fantasy that a philosopher could stay afloat by clinging to a spar of objectivity.

Temperamentally religious and inclined to believe in redemption (if not by faith then by literary works) Nietzsche failed to break the habit sanctioned by over two thousand years of philosophizing – the habit of worshipping the truth. The self-conquest he hoped to achieve in the new book is suggested in the first paragraph with a stern question that had probably never been posed: what is the value of the will to truth? Why should we not prefer untruth or uncertainty or ignorance? The answer is that we do. Our instinct for self-preservation teaches us to be superficial.

Calling himself an initiate of Dionysus, Nietzsche expounds 'the philosophy of this god', who often considers how to help man forward, 'and to make him stronger, more evil and more profound than he is'. (The cynicism counterbalances the sentimentality of believing in a benevolent deity.) Realizing that he had been ignoring the premises he had set out in his essay on truth and falsehood, Nietzsche resumes his argument about the impossibility of reporting accurately on external reality. Most conscious thinking must be discounted as an instinctive activity: falsification is a condition of our existence.

How can we feel confident to make any statement? Who is making it? How is it possible to say 'I think' or 'I will'? Descartes had been ignoring the body when he said: 'I think, therefore I am,' and had failed to answer the metaphysical questions he raised.

Where does the concept *thinking* derive from? Why do I believe in cause and effect? What gives me the right to speak of an 'I', and even of an 'I' as cause, and finally of an

'I' as cause of thought? ... Other people may assume that to know something is to know it wholly, but the philosopher must tell himself: when I analyse the process that is suggested by the sentence 'I think', I find a series of risky assertions, whose basis is difficult, perhaps impossible, to establish – for instance that it is *I* that am thinking, at least that there must be something which thinks, that thinking must be an activity and a function of a being which can be considered to be taking an initiative, that an *I* exists, and finally that what thinking means has already been established, that I *know* what thinking is. For if I have not already made my mind up about this, how can I calculate whether what is currently happening is not perhaps 'willing' or 'feeling'? In fact, the assertion 'I think' presupposes that to ascertain what my current state of mind is, I *compare* it with other states of mind which are familiar to me ... It is falsifying the facts to say that the subject 'I' is a condition of the predicate 'think'. A thought comes when 'it' wants, not when 'I' want ... 'It' thinks, but that this 'it' is identical with the good old 'I' is at best only an assumption.

Beyond Good and Evil, §§16–17

Presenting thought as no more than a relationship between various drives, Nietzsche had to picture himself in a state of Dionysian dispersal.

Dionysus was the god of masks (or *personae*) and to speak through them, Nietzsche needed a variety of voices. Without a mask one has no face to present, and it is only through masks that one can speak out what one has learnt. The mask can never be removed unless there is another mask behind it, and we write books not to reveal but to conceal what is inside us. Can a philosopher ever have 'final and genuine' opinions?

The man who sits in his cave, alone with his soul in confidential dialogue and dispute, year in, year out, day and night – whether the cave is a labyrinth or a goldmine – must become a cave bear or a treasure seeker or a guard and dragon; his ideas eventually acquire their own twilight colour, odours of both profundity and mustiness, something incommunicable and rebarbative, that blow out coldly at each passer-by. The hermit does not believe that a philosopher – assuming that every philosopher started as a hermit – can ever express his opinions conclusively in books. Are books not written in order to conceal what one has inside? Yes, the hermit will question whether a philosopher *can* have formed conclusions about anything, whether, for him, each cave leads – must lead – into another, deeper cave; each surface must conceal a fuller, stranger, richer world, while there must be a subsoil below the soil in which each argument is 'grounded'. In the hermit's opinion, all philosophies are foreground philosophies. 'There was something both arbitrary and suspect about his decision to stop at this point and survey what was behind him and around him, to throw down his spade instead of digging deeper *here*.' Every philosophy *conceals* another philosophy; every opinion is also a hiding-place, every word a *mask*.

Beyond Good and Evil, §289

Here Nietzsche is trying not to disguise his voice and not to wear any mask except the inevitable one of 'the philosopher' But to philosophize is to engage in didactic activity, and it is questionable whether this can be done without either a mask or a platform of stable identity.

Managing without masks and voices, Nietzsche is in greater danger of contradicting himself and of producing prose subject to noticeable changes in emotional temperature. His writing tends to become more rhetorical as more libido is involved. Though his habit of structuring books in relatively short sequences usually obviates the need to sustain long philosophical arguments, he tends to digress or change emotional gear when anger or admiration is aroused. The tone is far from neutral when he writes about the blond beast.

> Just suppose it were true – what now in any case is believed to be the 'truth' – that the *meaning of all culture* is to make that predatory animal, man, into a tame and civilized animal, to breed a domestic pet. Then what we would have to regard as the *instruments of culture* would indubitably be the instincts of reaction and *ressentiment*, which finally helped to discredit and overthrow the nobility and its values; which is not to say that the *bearers* of those impulses suddenly represent culture themselves. The opposite, rather, would not only appear to be possible – no, today it is patently obvious. The bearers of these depressing instincts are liable to provoke retaliation. Descended from all the European and non-European

slaves, and especially of the whole the pre-Aryan popula-
tion, these people represent the *regression* of humanity.

These 'instruments of culture' are a disgrace to humanity and a counter-argument against 'culture' in general. It
would be understandable if we cannot rid ourselves of our
fear of the blond beast at the core of all noble races, and if
we remain on our guard against it. But who would not a
hundred times rather be afraid and admire at the same
time than *not* be afraid and at the same time be unable to
get rid of the disgusting sight of those who are ill-bred,
stunted, deformed, poisoned? And is that not *our* fate?
What is causing our revulsion against *mankind*? For there
can be no doubt that we are suffering from *mankind*.

The Genealogy of Morals, First Essay, §11

Henry Staten, who is good at spotting and interpreting
unintended changes in tone, noticed how impassioned
Nietzsche became when discussing the type he calls the
aristocrat-priest. In the 1887 book *The Genealogy of Morals*,
his interest in the evolution of this type exerts 'a pull that
bends his prose into what is not progressive narration but an
oscillation, in a pattern not unlike that remarked by Derrida
in Freud's *Beyond the Pleasure Principle*. For the object by
which Nietzsche is fascinated, the object he keeps drawing
near and then pushing away, *the ascetic will*, is already fully
present in the aristocrat-priest with whom he begins his
account, and all Nietzsche's narratives of progressive development entwine themselves around the pulsations of his
fascination with and revulsion from this object.'

Concerned with the development of good and evil as

concepts, *The Genealogy of Morals* consists of three essays. The first is about the difference between 'bad' and 'evil' and about contrasting meanings of 'good' in the moralities of masters and slaves. Nietzsche overturns the unhistorical assumption of 'English psychologists' that the idea of goodness was originated by those who benefited from altruistic actions. The evolution of language had been determined by the dominant groups, who had used their name-giving prerogative to glorify themselves and their qualities, while denigrating those of other groups. 'Good' had been synonymous with 'noble', 'bad' with plebeian. In Homer the heroes are always noble, the commoners always feeble, contemptible or cunning. The association of 'highborn' with high-minded and 'low-born' with 'base' still survives in most languages.

Turning to the emergence of the priestly sect, Nietzsche suggests that its emphasis on cleanliness made abstinence into a virtue. The various lusts – for power, conquest, love-making, revenge – all came to seem dangerous, and man looked like an interesting animal because he had an opportunity offered to none of the other predatory beasts – he could sin. While the values of the warrior-leaders presupposed a healthy interest in fighting, hunting, adventure and dancing, the achievement of the priests was to poison the bloodstream: the Judaeo-Christian morality was a slave morality, the outcome of an ethical revolution fuelled by resentment – 'the *ressentiment* of those who are incapable of taking action and make up for it by means of an imaginary revenge'. The weak can feel superior to the strong, pitying them for what they will suffer in hell.

Though the priest and the slave are equally prone to this *ressentiment*, Nietzsche is ambivalent about priests and the kind of *ressentiment* they instil. Titled 'Guilt, Bad Conscience and the Like', the second essay explains bad conscience as the illness humanity had to contract when, undergoing a fundamental transformation, it found itself constricted by society and peace. Instincts that could not be released had to be turned inwards, while the whole inner world, 'originally as thin as if stretched between two membranes, expanded outwards and upwards, acquiring, depth, breadth and height as outward discharge was blocked'.

> Forced back into a latent state, this *instinct for freedom* – we already understand it – pushed backwards, retracted, turned inwards, until it can be released only against itself – this is the sole origin of *bad conscience*.
>
> One should be careful not to dismiss this whole phenomenon simply because it is thoroughly distasteful and painful. Fundamentally the same active force is at work on a larger scale in the organizers and artists in violence who build states. Internal, small, petty, directed backwards into what Goethe calls 'the labyrinth of the breast', the *instinct for freedom* (or, in my terminology, will to power) creates for itself bad conscience and forms negative ideals. But here, the material attacked by the form-building and violating nature of this force is man, his whole primeval animal self, and *not*, as in that greater and more obvious phenomenon, *another* man, *other* men. This secret self-ravishing, this artistic cruelty, this lust to impose form on oneself as on a tough, resistant, suffering

material, cauterizing into oneself a will, a criticism, a contradiction, a contempt, a negation; this uncanny, weirdly enjoyable labour of a voluntarily divided soul making itself suffer out of pleasure in causing suffering, finally this whole, *active* 'bad conscience' – you can guess already – as the true womb of all ideal and imaginative experience.

The Genealogy of Morals, Second Essay, §§17–18

The argument is confusing if we deny Nietzsche the right to contradict himself. Inferior to his masters, the ascetic priest had come under attack because his instincts were rooted in something unhealthy and because he made the sick masses sicker as their bad instincts coagulated into self-discipline. But self-discipline was beneficial to such a sick animal as man, whose

restless energy gives him no peace, making his future dig like a spur into each moment of his present – how could such a courageous and richly talented animal fail to be the most endangered, most deeply and desperately sick of all animals?

Though he had traced asceticism back to degeneration, Nietzsche exults in the 'restless energy' that drives humanity towards its future. In spite of himself, he admires the will that makes itself suffer in order to re-create itself.

But there is little point in reprimanding Nietzsche for inconsistency and for flouting the law of non-contradiction, which he despised. One of his achievements was to show that its value was limited. His attacks on language and logic were launched most cogently in work he left unpublished. His formulations of 1886–7 do not substantially diverge from those of the 1873 essay except in abandoning the distinction he had drawn between concepts and intuitive awareness. Though he often referred, as an empiricist would, to the evidence of the senses, for him the

> antithesis of the phenomenal world is not 'the real world' but the formless, unformulable world of the chaos of sensations – *another kind* of phenomenal world, 'unknowable' to us ... The fictitious world of subject, substance, 'reason' etc. is indispensable ... 'Truth' is the will to be master over the multiplicity of sensations ... In this ... we take phenomena as *real*.

> *The Will to Power*, §517

Being indescribable, the character of a world in a state of flux may seem false or self-contradictory. If language and logic can cope only with a fictional world in which everything remains static, the law of non-contradiction can be no more binding on us than, say, the rule of the three unities.

> The conceptual ban on contradiction proceeds from the assumption ... that the concept not only designates the essence of a thing but *comprehends* it ... Logic is an attempt to comprehend actuality by means of a scheme of being we have ourselves proposed.

> §516

There is little doubt that Nietzsche was mad for the last twelve years of his short life (1844–1900) but it is impossible to be sure when he went mad. It is not even easy to say when he first confronted the prospect of madness. His friend Franz Overbeck thought he had been 'living his way towards' the final breakdown, and at Basel University, when he was twenty-five, he wrote:

> What am I afraid of is not the frightful shape behind my chair but its voice; also not the words, but the identifying unarticulated and inhuman tone of that shape. Yes, if only it could speak as human beings do.
>
> *Notes from the years 1868–9*

This outcrop of delusionary language is isolated, but the emphasis on voice is significant, while the ideas of distribution, dispersal, disintegration were basic to his mental habits. He tried not to think in terms of individuals but of forces. The stable identity of the ego disappears, and the book he began in 1880, *Sunrise*, argues that even during the pre-Christian period, convention had been so relentlessly oppressive that madness had been a factor in the history of morality.

> Plato was speaking for the whole of humanity when he said: 'From madness Greece has derived its greatest benefits.' For those superior intellects who were irresistibly driven to break the yoke of a convention and make new laws, there was no alternative, *if they were not really mad*, but to feign madness.

If they were not brave enough to feign it, they must induce it, and the recipe Nietzsche jocularly offers is like a distorting mirror focused on the routine of his own life:

inordinate fasting, continual sexual abstinence, withdrawal into the wilderness, or climbing a mountain, or
onto a pillar, or 'sitting on an ancient willow facing a lake',
and thinking resolutely of nothing except what provokes
ecstasy and mental derangement.

The joke encourages the suspicions it may have been
intended to allay – that there was an element of self-
destructiveness in Nietzsche's lifestyle. His sexual abstinence
was mainly involuntary, but his diet, which was eccentric
and inadequate, was determined less by poverty than by
masochistic self-discipline. Physical comfort was less impor-
tant to him than ambition to be one of the great law-killers.
In all periods, he argues, the most creative men suffered the
most and, haunted by the law they killed, yearned for the
delirium that would enable them to think themselves above
it. St Paul was one of those law-killers, and Nietzsche's
denunciation of him was based at least partly on fellow-
feeling, just as later, when he wrote about the death of God,
he was thinking about the death of divine law and feeling
remorse at having been one of the assassins.

But to be a legislator is to be a leader, and even when he
was speaking through the mouth of the prophet he had
invented, Zarathustra, Nietzsche had misgivings, which he
passed straight on to Zarathustra.

Do you know the terror that comes while falling asleep?
    The fear reaches right down to the toes as the ground
seems to give way and the dream begins.
    I give you this by way of a parable. Yesterday at the

stillest hour, the ground moved under my feet and the dream began.

The clock of my life held its breath as the hand moved on – never had I heard such silence all round me, and it frightened my heart.

Then it spoke with no voice: *'You know it, Zarathustra?'*

And I cried out in fear at this whisper, and the blood drained from my face, but I kept silent.

It spoke again with no voice: 'You know it, Zarathustra, but you say it not!'

And I finally answered like one who is headstrong: 'Yes, I know it but do not want to say it.'...

Then it again spoke voicelessly: 'What do you know of *that*? The dew falls on the grass when the night is most deeply silent.'

And I answered: You mocked me when I found my own way and went, and truly my feet were trembling then.'

And they told me this: You have forgotten the way and now you are forgetting how to walk!

Then it spoke voicelessly again: 'What does mockery matter? You are one who has forgotten how to obey. Now you should command!

Do you not know who is most needed by everyone? He who commands great deeds.

To perform great deeds is hard, but it is hardest of all to command them.

What is most unforgivable in you: you have the power to rule but not the desire.'

And I answered: 'I am no lion to roar commands.'

Again it spoke to me like a whisper: 'It is the softest words bring on the storm. The thoughts that steer the world come on the feet of doves.

Oh, Zarathustra, you must go as a shadow of what must come. In this way will you give commands and by commanding lead the way.'

And I answered: 'I am ashamed.'

Then it spoke again without a voice: 'Become a child once more and feel no shame.

The pride of youth is still on you. You have grown young late, but to become a child, conquer your youth.'

I thought for a long time and trembled. But finally I said what I had said at first: 'I do not want to.'

Then I heard laughter around me. Oh, how this laughter tore into my entrails and my heart.

And it spoke to me for the last time. 'Oh, Zarathustra, your fruits are ripe, but you are not ripe for your fruits!

So you must return to your solitude, for you have yet to become mellow.'

Zarathustra, Part Two, 'The Stillest Hour'

One of the luxuries *Zarathustra* offered Nietzsche was the opportunity to imagine that he had disciples and an audience for his preaching. He could even entertain fantasies of preparing them for battle.

My brothers in war! I love you utterly, I am and was one of your kind. And I am also your best enemy. So let me tell you the truth.

I know about the hatred and envy in your hearts. You

48

are not great enough not to know hatred and envy. So be great enough not to be ashamed of them.

And if you cannot be saints of knowledge, be at least its warriors. They are the companions and forerunners of this saintliness.

I see many soldiers; I would like to see many warriors. What they wear is called uniform; what they cover with it should not be uniform.

You should be men whose eyes always reach for enemies – *your* enemies. And some of you hate at first sight. Your enemy you should seek, your war you should wage, and for your ideas. And if your ideas are defeated, then your honesty should still celebrate the triumph!

You should love peace as the way to new wars, finding brief interludes of peace preferable to long ones.

To you I do not commend work but battles. To you I do not commend peace but victory. Let your work be a battle, your peace a victory.

One can be silent and sit still only when one has a bow and arrow: otherwise one chatters and quarrels. Your peace should be a victory.

You say that a good cause justifies even war? I say unto you: it is a good war that justifies any cause.

Zarathustra, Part One, 'On War and Warriors'

But Nietzsche had no disciples and only a small audience for his books. Isolation was acting like a slow poison on his sanity, but it was only in the final phase of his work that delusions of grandeur were seriously damaging.

There was nothing pathological about his realization that

in a godless world, humanity would need a new morality, but it was insane to think it could be supplied *in toto* by a single philosopher. On 3 September 1888 Nietzsche wrote what he intended as the preface to the first volume of his *Transvaluation of All Values* – 'perhaps the proudest preface ever written'.

> This book belongs to the few. Perhaps none of them are even alive yet. It may be those who understand my *Zarathustra*: how *could* I confuse myself with those who can already find an audience? Only the day after tomorrow belongs to me. Some are born posthumously ...

Among the prerequisites for understanding him were habituation to mountain altitudes and to

> seeing the pitiful gossip about politics and national interest *from above* ... The brave man's predilection for questions that intimidate his contemporaries, courage for the forbidden ... A new conscience for truths which have kept silent ... Reverence for oneself, love for oneself, unlimited freedom with oneself.
>
> Preface to *The Anti-Christ*

In a letter to a friend, he announced that as soon as the book had been read and understood

> it will split the history of mankind into two halves ... Much that has been free will be free no longer: the realm of *tolerance* is reduced by value judgments of the first importance to mere cowardice and feebleness of character. To be a Christian – I am mentioning just one

consequence – will from then on be *indecent*. A great deal of this, the most radical subversion humanity has ever known, is already under way inside me.

Letter to Paul Deussen, 14 Sept. 1888

Instead of embarking on a transvaluation of all values, the book that follows this proud preface, *The Anti-Christ*, reiterates points Nietzsche had already made about power, weakness, decadence, pity and the Judaeo-Christian morality. But by now he was incapable of self-criticism. The book was half-finished when he claimed:

It has an energy and transparency which have perhaps never been achieved by a philosopher. It seems to me as though all at once I have learned how to *write* ... The work cuts clean through the centuries. I swear that everything which has been said or thought in criticism of Christianity is pure childishness in comparison.

Letter to Franz Overbeck, Sept. 1888

Delusions of grandeur were making Nietzsche peremptory with his friends. To one who diplomatically expressed dissent with his pamphlet *The Case of Wagner* he wrote:

These are not things on which I tolerate contradiction. On questions of decadence I am the highest court of appeal there is on earth. Present-day humanity, with its wretchedly vitiated instincts, should think itself lucky to have someone who can pour out clean wine.

Letter to Malwida von Meysenbug, 18 Oct. 1888

The strategies he adopted to achieve self-sufficiency

became increasingly desperate. Alone on his forty-fourth birthday, he celebrated by starting the book *Ecce Homo*.

> Seeing that before long I must confront humanity with the gravest demand ever made on it, it seems essential to say *who I am* ... The disproportion between the greatness of my task and the *smallness* of my contemporaries has found expression in their having neither heard nor seen me.

He goes on to praise *Zarathustra* as the highest and deepest book in existence,

> an inexhaustible spring into which no bucket descends without coming back laden with gold and goodness ... It is an incomparable privilege to be a listener here ... It was not in vain today that I buried my forty-fourth year. I was entitled to bury it – whatever life there was in it is saved, is immortal.
>
> *Ecce Homo*, Preface and Epigraph

Such chapter headings as 'Why I Am So Wise' and 'Why I Write Such Good Books' could hardly fail to irritate, but the final section, 'Why I Am Destiny' looks impressively at the future. Though he was no nihilist, he comes close to facing the consequences of his wish to annihilate mediocrity when the vast bulk of humanity is irredeemably mediocre. What will happen now he has cut the lifeline of lies that Judaism and Christianity held out?

> One day my name will be associated with something catastrophic – a crisis such as there has never been on

earth, the most profound collision of conscience. I am not a man, I am dynamite ... When truth starts battling with the lies of millennia, we shall have convulsions, a spasm of earthquakes, a displacement of mountain and valley such as no-one has ever dreamed of ... The concept of politics will be assimilated wholly into ideological warfare, all the power structures of the old society will be blown up – they are all founded on lies. There will be wars such as there have never been on earth.

Ecco Homo, 'Why I am Destiny', §1

He had reached the point of confusing mental images and literary activity with external events. Ten days after finishing this chapter he wrote:

Considering what I have written between 3 September and 4 November, I fear there may soon be a small earthquake ... two years ago, when I was in Nice, it happened, appropriately, there. Indeed, yesterday's report from the observatory mentioned a small tremor.

Letter to Meta von Salis, 14 Nov. 1888

By December he was manically confident that nothing was beyond his powers.

The most unheard-of tasks are easy as a game; my health like the weather, coming up daily with boundless brilliance and assurance. The world will be inverted for the next few years: since the old god has abdicated, I shall be ruling the world.

Letter to Carl Fuchs, 11 Dec. 1888

No longer having editorial control over statements made by voices in his head, Nietzsche could no longer be sure of his identity. The last of his letters with his own name in the signature was written to the Swedish playwright August Strindberg at the end of the year: 'I have ordered a convocation of princes in Rome. I want to have the young Kaiser shot.' The signature was 'Nietzsche Caesar'. We could now say of him what Jung said about his spiritualist cousin: repressed elements had erupted into hallucinations as if they were independent personalities.

Sending Nietzsche a letter that was written entirely in Greek and Latin, Strindberg started with a quotation from an Anacreontic poem – 'I want, I want to be mad.' The letter, which ended 'Meanwhile it is a joy to be mad', was signed: 'Strindberg (Deus, optimus maximus)'.

On the morning of 3 January 1889 Nietzsche saw a cab driver beating his horse in a piazza. Tearfully the philosopher threw his arms around the animal's neck, and collapsed. Later, taken to an asylum, he thought Wagner's widow, Cosima, had brought him there, and he was confused about his identity, sometimes calling himself the Duke of Cumberland or the Kaiser, and once saying: 'I was Friedrich Wilhelm IV the last time.' He sometimes spoke in French to other patients, and thought the chief warder was Bismarck.

Three of the letters Nietzsche wrote at the beginning of January 1889 are signed 'Dionysus', and three are signed 'The Crucified'. He wrote to the King of Italy, addressing him as 'My beloved Umberto' and to the Vatican Secretary of State. In another letter he said:

The world is transfigured for God is on the earth. Do you not see how all the heavens are rejoicing? I have just seized possession of my kingdom, am throwing the pope into prison and having Wilhelm, Bismarck and Stocker shot.

In a letter he posted on 5 January he wrote:

Actually I would much rather be a Basel professor than God, but I have not ventured to carry my private egoism so far as to desist from creating the world on his account. You see, one must make sacrifices, however one may be living, and wherever ... Since I am condemned to while away the next eternity with bad jokes, I have a writing business here which really leaves nothing to be desired – very pleasant and not at all exhausting. The unpleasant thing, which offends my modesty, is that fundamentally I am every name in history. As for the children I have brought into the world, I have to consider with some suspicion whether all those who enter the 'Kingdom of God' do not also come out of God.

Letter to Jakob Burckhardt, dated 6 Jan. 1889
                                        but posted on the 5th

He was to survive for over eleven years, which he spent in a state of supinity. A musician, Peter Gast, who visited him in January 1890 formed the impression that 'his mental disturbance consists of no more than a heightening of the humorous antics he used to put on for an intimate circle of friends', but when Gast took him out for walks, it was obvious he had no desire to resume his former life. 'It seemed – horrible through this is – as if Nietzsche were merely feigning madness, as if he were glad for it to have ended in this way.' This tallies with the findings of Franz Overbeck, who arrived in February. 'I cannot escape the ghastly suspicion ... that his madness is simulated. This impression can be explained only by the experiences I have had of Nietzsche's self-concealments, of his spiritual masks.'

But he rarely came out with a coherent sentence. On 1 February, when Gast arrived with six doughnuts, Nietzsche said: 'No, my friend, I do not want to get sticky fingers now, because I want to play a little first.' And he sat down at the piano to improvise. 'Not one wrong note! Interweaving tones of Tristan-like sensitivity ... Beethoven-like profundity and jubilant songs rising above it. Then again reveries and dreams.' Unable or unwilling to use masks or voices, he could still communicate through music.

The aetiology of his illness and his madness are problematic: contemporary diagnoses are unreliable and the surviving evidence is scanty. Though his father suffered from epileptic attacks (probably *petit mal*) we cannot be certain that these were syphilitic, or that Nietzsche's childhood illnesses were hereditary. His headaches may have been due to sinositis, which can cause persistent and chronic discomfort if not effectively treated, while it can hardly have been hereditary syphilis that drove Nietzsche mad, or the breakdown would have occurred earlier. In January 1889, after the onset of madness, he said he had infected himself twice in 1866. If a Leipzig doctor diagnosed venereal disease, he was probably basing his opinion on sores, and he may have been wrong.

We know Nietzsche went to a brothel in 1865, but apparently he left without even touching any of the girls. Thomas Mann conjectured that he went back, but this seems unlikely. Since we cannot be sure that the final madness was syphilitic, there is no need to assume that Nietzsche must somehow or other have infected himself with syphilis. Apart from his own statements, made after he went mad, there is no evidence that he ever made love to a woman – or a man.

We cannot exclude the possibility of cerebral syphilis, which may have caused the stroke he suffered in 1898, but it is improbable that the delusions of grandeur or the breakdown had anything to do with syphilis. For many years between the breakdown and the stroke, Nietzsche remained free from incontinence and from any serious bodily paralysis, while he retained at least partial control over his memory. His mother could look after him almost unaided, and he could still speak without any slurring. None of this can be reconciled easily with the diagnosis of *dementia paralytica*. Nor can I find any evidence for the rumour, which both Freud and Jung helped to propagate, that he visited a Genoese male brothel.

With his headaches, his eye trouble, his vomiting and his madness, he was, more directly than any other thinker, living out the consequences of moving away from organized religion. The relevance of his experience is all the greater if the causes of his collapse were not organic. There is often an element of choice in breakdowns and a histrionic element in madness, though it seems improbable that Nietzsche was merely faking or that he would have gone to such lengths just to escape the humiliation of having failed to revalue all values. He had anticipated his own fate in a note on 'the last philosopher'. His way of saying 'Grant oblivion' was to break down.

But Nietzsche's madness invalidates neither his philosophical achievements nor the demand he was making on us. If we follow him into the *impasse*, we cannot escape in the way he did. We may get acclimatized to God's absence, but if we lose faith in language and truth, how are we to communicate? If we lose faith in the coherence of the self, how can we know who is thinking when we do? Over a century has passed since Nietzsche challenged the assumptions behind all our conventions, but we have found neither answers nor alternative conventions.